DATE DUE			

615014 01822   21690C   044

KALEIDOSCOPE

THE
LUNGS

by
Suzanne LeVert

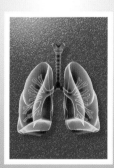

BENCHMARK BOOKS

MARSHALL CAVENDISH
NEW YORK

Benchmark Books
Marshall Cavendish Corporation
99 White Plains Road
Tarrytown, NY 10591-9001
Website: www.marshallcavendish.com

Library of Congress Cataloging-in-Publication Data.

LeVert, Suzanne.
The lungs / by Suzanne LeVert.
   p.cm. – (Kaleidoscope)
Includes bibliographical references and index.
ISBN 0-7614-1307-3
1. Lungs—Juvenile literature. [1. Lungs.] I. Title. II. Series.
QP121..L455 2001   612.2—dc21   00-050726

Photo Research by Anne Burns Images

Cover by Alfred Pasieka/Science Photo Library

All photos used in this book are used with the permission of: *Photo Edit:* Allan Oddie, 5; Marleen Cate, 24; Tony Freeman, 28, 43; Spencer Grant, 31. Marleen Ferguson, 32. Mary Kaye Denny, 35. D. Young-Wolf, 39. *Photo Researchers:* Dr. Michael Smith, Milton S. Hershey Medical Centre/Science Photo Library, 6. Science Photo Library, 9. Scott Camazine, 14. Gary Carlson, 17. Porf. P. Motta/ G Macciarelli University "La Sapienza" Rome/ Science Photo Library, 18, 27. John Bavosi/Science Photo Library, 21. Biophoto Associates, 22. *Phototake:* Jane Hurd, 10. Martin Rotker, 40. *Peter Arnold:* Matt Meadows, 13. Alfred Pasieka, 36.

Printed in Italy

6 5 4 3 2 1

CONTENTS

THE BREATH OF LIFE   4

THE LUNGS   7

THE ART OF BREATHING   23

LET'S TALK DEFENSE   26

MAKING NOISE   29

WHAT CAN GO WRONG   34

KEEP BREATHING DEEP!   41

GLOSSARY   44

FIND OUT MORE   46

INDEX   48

THE BREATH OF LIFE

Breathe in as deeply as you can. Watch your chest rise as your lungs fill with air, then fall as you exhale. Now, hold your breath for just a few seconds. Do you feel how much you want to take a gulp of air? That's because the oxygen in the air is vital to life, and it is the job of your lungs and respiratory system to provide oxygen for all the cells in the body. Just as important is the job they do of getting rid of carbon dioxide, a waste gas of the body that you exhale with every breath. This system also makes it possible for you to talk and sing. Let's take a look at how this process works.

A doctor listens to a young boy's lungs with a stethoscope.

4

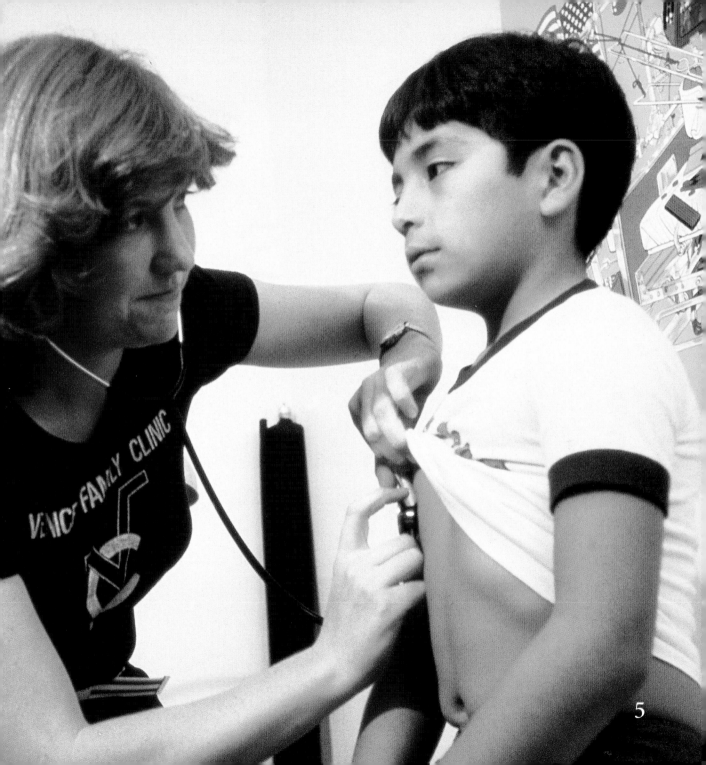

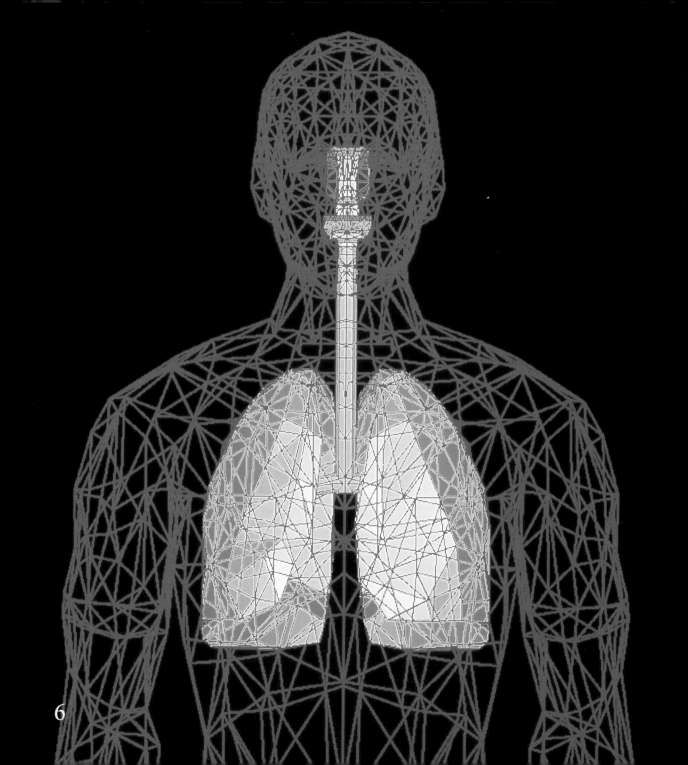

6

THE LUNGS

When you breathe in, your lungs take in oxygen from the air and send it to the cells of the body via the bloodstream. When you exhale, your lungs expel carbon dioxide, one of the body's major waste products. Each lung expands (becomes larger) and contracts (becomes smaller), between twelve and twenty times every minute, every hour, for every day of your life.

Air is breathed into the nose and mouth and passed down the pharynx before entering the trachea. The two lungs (in green) are the main organs of the respiratory system.

You have two lungs, one on each side of your chest. Bones called ribs surround and protect your lungs and other vital organs. A membrane called the *pleura* covers the outside of the lungs and the chest wall. This membrane allows your lungs to move easily within the chest as you breathe.

 Your right and left lungs are protected by your rib cage.

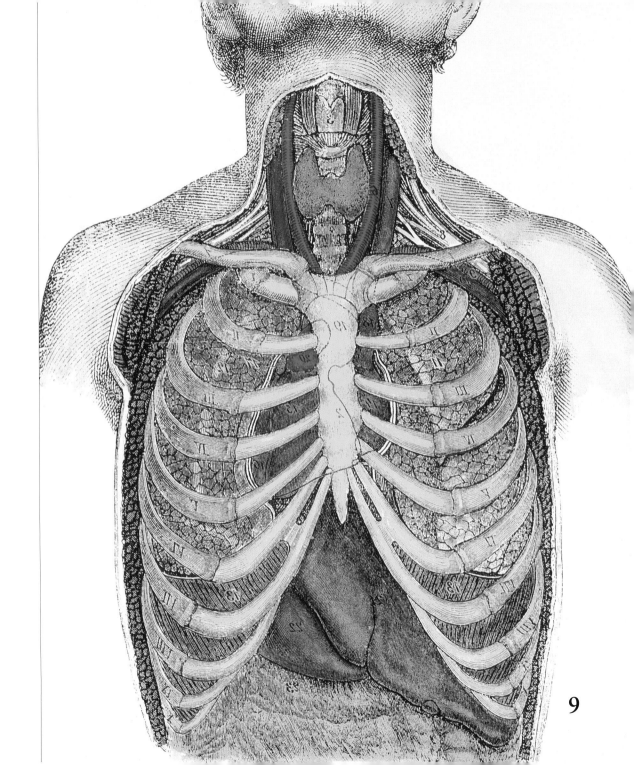

9

LUNGS

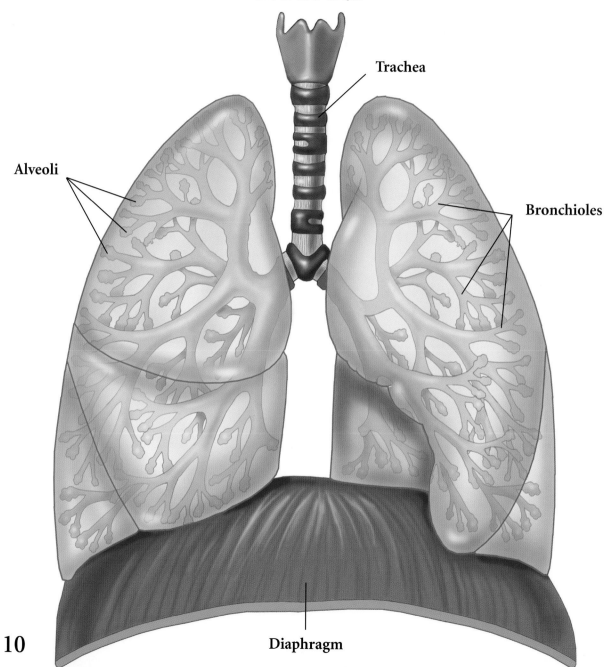

Trachea

Alveoli

Bronchioles

Diaphragm

10

Together, the lungs form one of the largest organs in the body. Your two lungs are not exactly the same. The right one has three sections, or lobes. The left one has only two lobes and a hollowed-out area where the heart sits. The tops of your lungs reach above your collarbone, almost to your neck. The bases of your lungs rest on the dome-shaped breathing muscle called the *diaphragm,* which sits on top of your stomach.

The lungs are made up of sections of tissue called lobes. They are soft and spongy, and ready to fill up with air.

Inside Your Lungs

Your lungs are soft and spongy. But instead of soaking up water like a sponge does, they fill up with air. If you are healthy, your lungs are a pinkish gray color, but even healthy lungs can become blackened from particles in the polluted air you breathe.

Healthy human lungs.

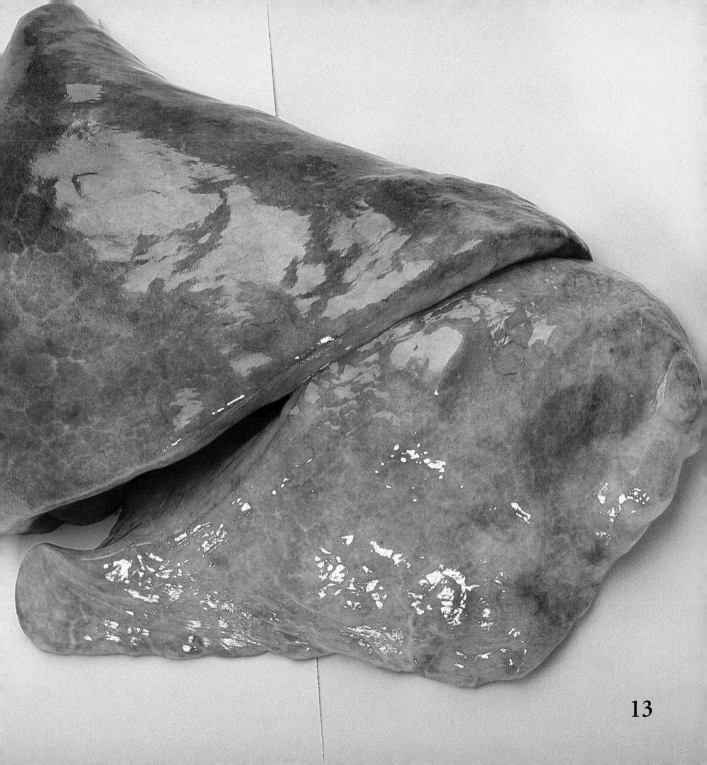

13

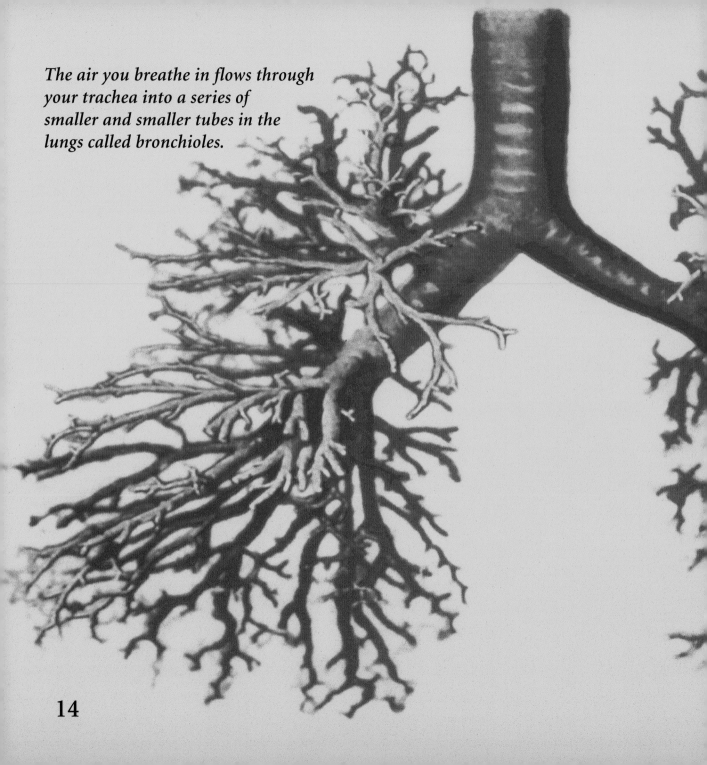

The air you breathe in flows through your trachea into a series of smaller and smaller tubes in the lungs called bronchioles.

14

Air first enters through your mouth and nose, then travels through the back of your throat, through your voice box (called the *larynx*), and down your windpipe (called the *trachea*). The trachea branches into two main air passageways called bronchial tubes, or bronchi. Inside your lungs, the bronchi branch off into smaller and smaller tubes, forming what looks like an upside down tree.

15

The smallest of these tubes, called the *bronchioles*, look like tiny twigs of a vine bearing bunches of grapes. The "grapes" are groups of small air sacs called *alveoli*. The alveoli are where the oxygen enters the bloodstream. You have about 300 million alveoli inside each of your lungs. If you stretched them out on a flat surface, they would cover an area about the size of a tennis court.

Air sacs containing oxygen—called alveoli—cover the bronchioles. Oxygen enters the bloodstream from the alveoli.

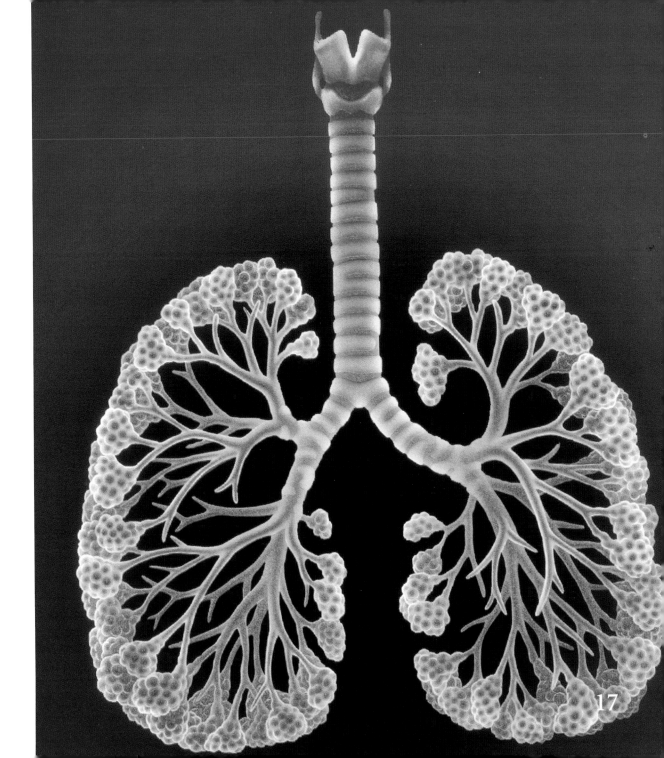

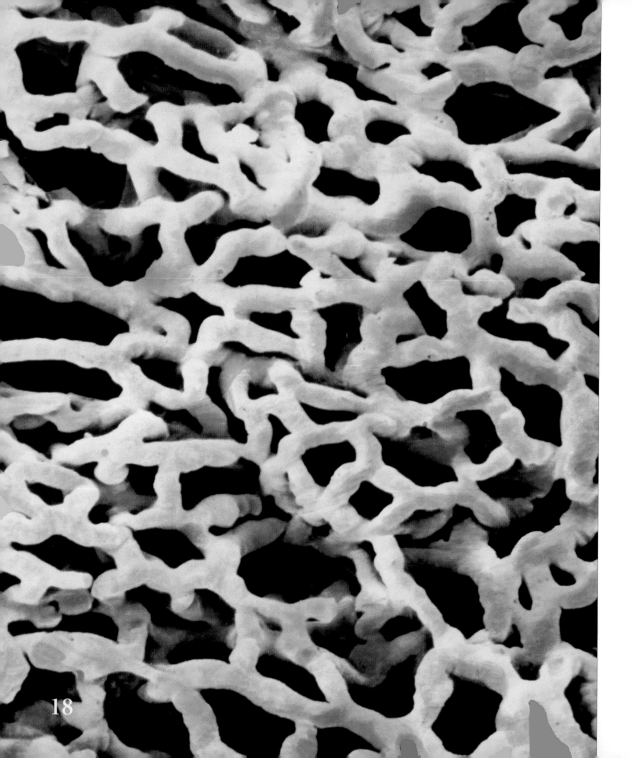

18

The alveoli are made of only a single or double layer of cells. Tiny blood *vessels* called *capillaries* wrap around the alveoli. This makes it easy for oxygen to enter the bloodstream, and for the blood to get rid of its waste gas, carbon dioxide.

The network of capillaries in the lungs that surround the alveoli, where the exchange of gases and blood occurs.

Your Lungs and Your Heart

Your lungs are connected to your heart by blood vessels called pulmonary *veins* and *arteries.* The word "pulmonary" comes from the Latin word *pulmo,* which means "lung". Your blood travels through your body, giving up oxygen and gathering carbon dioxide, and returns to your heart through the pulmonary veins. When your blood has more carbon dioxide than oxygen in it, it appears to be a blue color. Your heart pumps this deoxygenated blue blood through the pulmonary artery to your lungs. The blood then passes through the arteries of the lungs into smaller and smaller vessels. Finally, it flows into the capillaries that sit next to the alveoli. Gases, such as oxygen and carbon dioxide, pass to and from the alveoli to the capillaries and gases are exchanged. When your blood has more oxygen in it than carbon dioxide, it takes on a bright red color. This blood is then pumped back into the heart and through the body, delivering oxygen to all the cells.

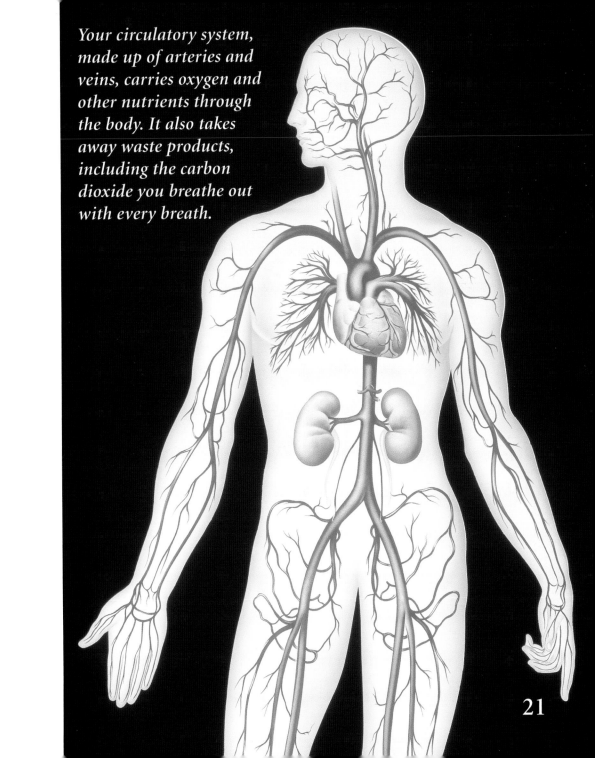

Your circulatory system, made up of arteries and veins, carries oxygen and other nutrients through the body. It also takes away waste products, including the carbon dioxide you breathe out with every breath.

21

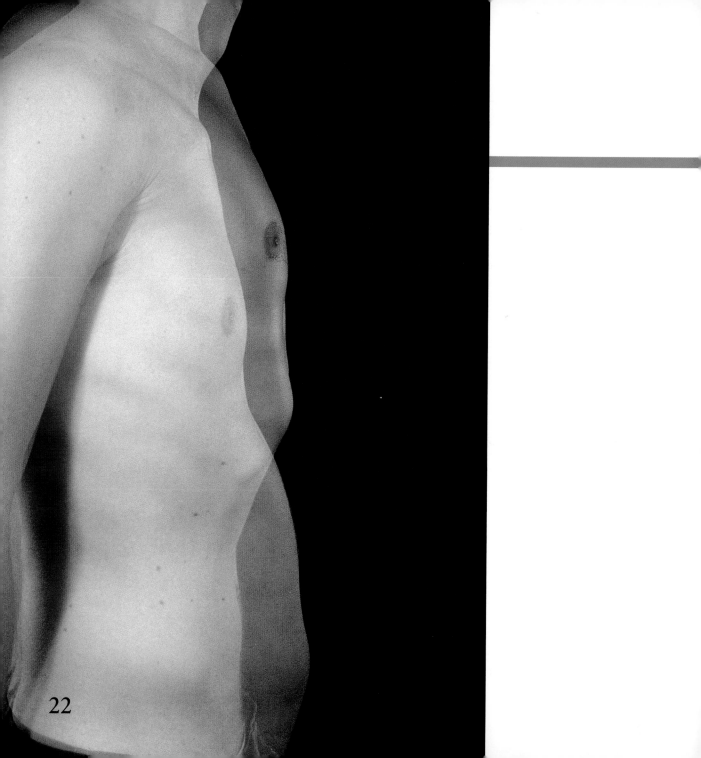

22

THE ART OF BREATHING

When you inhale, the muscles of your ribs contract, causing your ribs to move up and out. At the same time, your diaphragm contracts, pushing down toward your abdomen. This makes room for your chest cavity and lungs to expand as air rushes into the lungs. When you exhale, these muscles relax. The pressure from the abdomen below pushes your diaphragm back up. This makes the size of your chest cavity smaller and your lungs squeeze the stale air, now carrying carbon dioxide, out of your body.

The muscles of the chest and abdomen aid in breathing. When you inhale and exhale you can see your chest rise and fall.

As you sit here quietly reading this book, you're breathing in about one pint of air every fifteen seconds. When you run or ride your bike, though, your breathing rate can almost double. You also breathe more deeply so that you take in almost five times as much air.

 When you exercise, your brain and your muscles need more oxygen to work, so you take deeper and faster breaths.

LET'S TALK DEFENSE

Your respiratory system has several ways to protect itself from germs and other foreign material getting into your lungs. Hairs in your nose filter out the larger particles. Special cells in your airways secrete a sticky liquid called mucus that catches bacteria, dust, and other material. Mucus also moistens dry air so that it doesn't dry out your lungs. Tiny hairlike growths called *cilia* line your airways. These cilia continuously beat the mucus upward toward your throat to help keep the passageway to your lungs clear.

Tiny hairlike growths called cilia line your airways. They flutter continuously, keeping the airways clear.

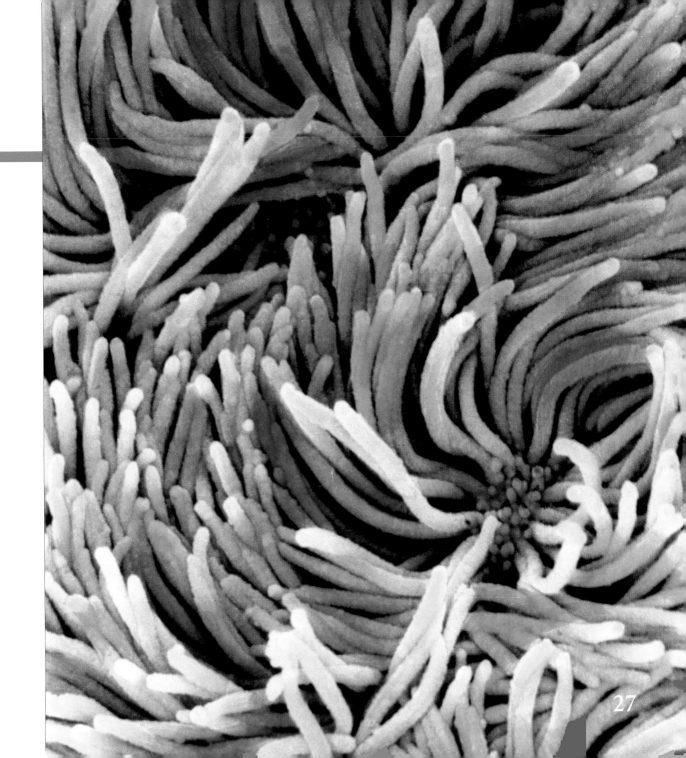

MAKING NOISE

Your vocal cords are two bands of fibrous tissue found at the base of the throat. You make sounds when air passes through tightened vocal cords. The greater the tension in your vocal cords, the higher the pitch of the sound you make. The harder you breathe out, the louder the sounds you make. Try it yourself and see! The different positions of your tongue, teeth, cheeks, and lips form the sounds into words.

The shape of your mouth and the tension you put on your vocal cords that determines the sounds you make when you speak, laugh, and yell. Try making different faces when you speak to see how you sound.

Coughing

Have you ever gotten food stuck in your throat? Then you know what it is like to have your brain trigger you to cough. Your lungs are very efficient at getting rid of unwanted material. If you inhale foreign particles, or if your airways become filled with too much mucus, nerve cells in the airways tell the brain. The brain then triggers you to cough. When you cough, you expel the material that is causing the irritation.

Covering your mouth when you cough isn't only polite, it also helps keep you from spreading unwanted germs and particles.

Hiccups

You've had the hiccups, haven't you? But do you know what causes the hiccup sound? Hiccups happen when your diaphragm—your main breathing muscle—suddenly contracts, which triggers your voice box to close sharply to stop the inflow of air. That causes you to make the hiccup sound. Hiccups usually clear up on their own, but drinking a glass of water or holding your breath for a few moments can sometimes help.

Holding your breath when you have the hiccups can help calm down the diaphragm, the muscle in the abdomen that causes hiccups when it becomes irritated.

33

WHAT CAN GO WRONG

Most of the time we don't think about having to breathe. It's one of those activities that our bodies carry on automatically. However, there are many common conditions and illnesses that may interfere with your ability to breathe.

• **The Common Cold**: If you are like most kids, you suffer from a stuffy, runny nose, a cough, and sneezing at least once or twice a year. Scientists have identified more than two hundred different viruses that cause a cold. Colds may not feel great, but they are not dangerous. They usually pass on their own within a week or so.

Having a cold is no fun—your lungs and nose become stuffed up, making it difficult to breathe.

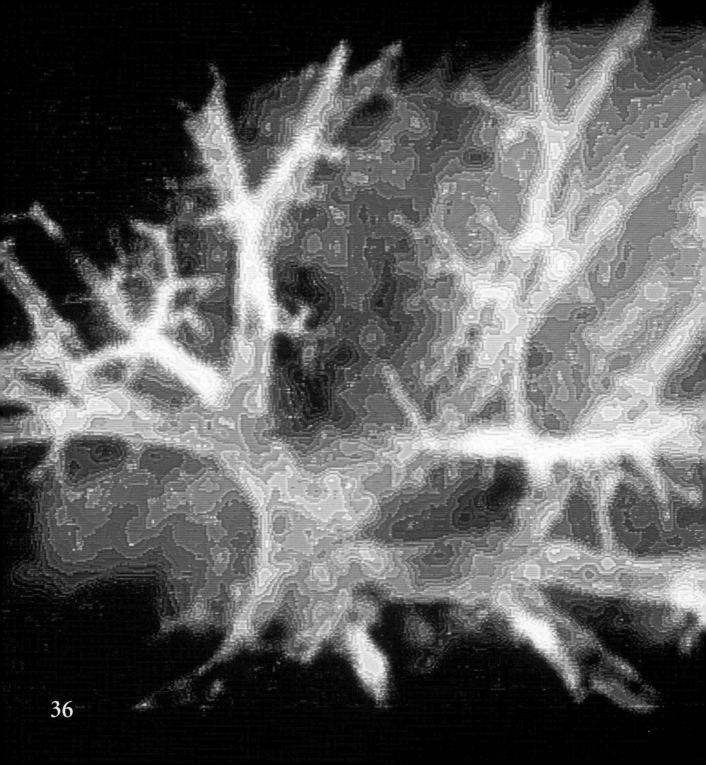

36

· **Bronchitis:** Sometimes your bronchi, or main breathing tubes, become inflamed, usually because of a cold or other respiratory infection. This disease produces symptoms that include a deep cough, a fever, and sometimes a slight wheeze because of clogged air passages. Chronic bronchitis is a condition usually caused by exposure to chemicals and other particles called *pollutants*, such as cigarette smoke. Coughing, throat irritation, and other symptoms can last longer than a cold.

Bronchitis is a condition in which your breathing tubes become swollen and inflamed, usually during an infection combined with the cold virus.

37

• **Asthma:** Chances are, you know someone with asthma because more than four million children under the age of sixteen have the disease. Asthma occurs when your breathing tubes become overly sensitive and close up. That causes a tight feeling in the chest, difficulty breathing, and wheezing. Respiratory infections, exercise, and allergies to dogs, cats, and other substances can cause or aggravate the condition. Many kids who have asthma use an inhaler filled with medicine to open up the air passages. Although some people have asthma throughout their lives, many people grow out of it during their teen years.

Asthma is a common condition among children. The breathing tubes become overly sensitive to certain particles in the air, like pollen and pet dander. Inhalers like the one this girl is using helps clear the air passages so breathing can occur normally.

Smoking cigarettes is lethal to your lungs. As you can see, the normally healthy pink lungs turn black and hard, making it difficult for them to take in air. Smoking causes serious illnesses like lung cancer and emphysema.

KEEP BREATHING DEEP!

Keeping your lungs and respiratory system as healthy as possible is an important goal. After all, they are responsible for providing each cell of your body with essential oxygen, removing body wastes, protecting you against infection, and providing you with the air you need in order to speak.

The most important thing you can do to keep your lungs strong and healthy is to never, never start smoking. Cigarette smoking damages your respiratory system, which leaves it more open to all kinds of infections. It destroys lung tissues, making it more difficult for you to breathe. And it even causes one of the deadliest cancers around, lung cancer.

It's almost impossible to avoid getting colds or other respiratory infections now and then. But you can cut down on your chances by washing your hands often and staying away from other kids who are sick. Eating a healthy diet and getting plenty of rest will also help. Like every other part of the body, your respiratory system also works best when you exercise it. Exercise helps to keep air passages open, the diaphragm strong, and your heart pumping.

The more exercise you get, the healthier your lungs and respiratory system will stay.

GLOSSARY

Alveoli   tiny air sacs in the lungs

Arteries   blood vessels that carry oxygen-filled blood to the rest of the body

Bronchioles   small air tubes in the lungs

Capillaries   the smallest blood vessels in the body

Cilia   hair like growths in the nose and in the air tubes

Diaphragm   the muscle that separates the abdomen from the chest and aids in breathing

Larynx   also known as the "voice box," it holds the vocal cords and the muscles that produce sound when you speak

Pleura   the thin membrane that covers both the lungs and the chest cavity

Pollutant   any substance that contaminates, or dirties, another

Trachea   also known as the windpipe, the trachea connects the throat to the bronchial tubes that carry air in the lungs

Veins   blood vessels that carry blood back to the heart

Vessels   tubes that carry blood and other substances throughout the body

FIND OUT MORE

BOOKS

Clayman, Charles, ed. *The Human Body: An Illustrated Guide to Its Structure, Function, and Disorders.* London: Dorling Kindersley, 1995

Sandeman, Anna. *The Children's Book of the Body.* Brookfield, CT: Cooper Beech Books, 1996

Parker, Steve. *The Lungs and Respiratory System.* Austin, TX: Raintree Steck-Vaughan, 1997

Humphrey, Elaine, et. al. *3D Lungs and Micro Tongues.* Somerville House USA, 2000

WEBSITES

KidsHealth
http://kidshealth.org/

The American Lung Association
http://www.lungusa.org/

AUTHOR'S BIO

Suzanne LeVert is a writer and editor of young adult and trade books with more than 30 titles to her credit. Although she specializes in health topics, Suzanne also enjoys writing about history and politics, and is the author of *Louisiana* and *Massachusetts* in the Benchmark Books series Celebrate the States. Suzanne currently lives in New Orleans and attends Tulane Law School.

INDEX

Page numbers for illustrations are in boldface.

abdomen, 23
air pollution, 12
airways, **14–15**, 15, 26, **27**, 30, 37, 42
allergies, 38
alveoli, 16–19, **17**, 20, 44
arteries, 20, 44
asthma, 38, **39**

blood, 19, 20
blood vessels, 44
blue blood, 20
breathing, 4, 7, 23–25, 41
bronchi, **14–15**, 15
bronchioles, **14–15**, 16, 44
bronchitis, **36**, 37

cancer, 41
capillaries, **18**, 19, 20, 44
carbon dioxide, 4, 7, 19, 20
cigarette smoke, 12, 37, **40**, 41
cilia, 26, **27**, 44
circulatory system, **21**
colds, 34, **35**, 37
color
    of blood, 20
    of lungs, 12, **40**
coughing, 30, **31**, 37

diaphragm, **10**, 11, 23, 33, 42, 44

exercise, **24**, 25, 38, 42, **43**
exhalation, 4, 7, 23

filters, 26
foreign particles, 26, 30, 37, 38

germs, 26, **31**

health habits, 42–43
hiccups, **32**, 33

infections, 34, 38, 41, 42
inflammation, 37
inhalation, 4, 7, 23
inhalers, **39**

larynx (voice box), 15, 33, 44
lobes, **10**, 11
location, 11
lungs, 6, **10**, **13**
    right and left, 11

mucus, 26, 30
muscles, **10**, 11, **23**, 33

nose, 26
nutrition, 42

oxygen, 4, 19, 25

pharynx, **6**
pleura, 8, 44
politeness, **31**
pollutants, 37
protection, 8, **9**, 26, **27**
pulmonary, 20

rib cage, 8, **9**

shape, **10**, 11
sickness, 34–41, **35**, **40**
size, 11, 16
sound, **28**, 29
speaking, **28**, 29
stethoscope, **5**

texture, 11, 12
throat irritation, 37
tightness, 38
trachea, **6**, 44

veins, 20, 44
viruses, 34, 37
vocal chords, 29

waste products. *See* carbon dioxide
Websites, 47
wheezing, 37, 38